This book belongs to

_____

Date

_____

God Speaks

40 Letters from the Father's Heart

Ruth O'Reilly-Smith

Authentic

Unless otherwise indicated, all Scripture quotations are taken from the Holy Bible,
New Living Translation, copyright © 1996, 2004, 2015 by Tyndale House Foundation.
Used by permission of Tyndale House Publishers, Carol Stream, Illinois 60188.
All rights reserved.

Scripture quotations marked (NIV) are taken from
The Holy Bible, New International Version Anglicised
Copyright © 1979, 1984, 2011 Biblica
Used by permission of Hodder & Stoughton Ltd, an Hachette UK company.
All rights reserved.
'NIV' is a registered trademark of Biblica
UK trademark number 1448790.

Scripture quotations marked (WEB) are from the World English Bible. 'World English
Bible' is a trademark.

Cover design by Emily Kelly Designs
emilykellydesigns.com

Printed and bound by Bell and Bain Ltd, Glasgow

Father God, thank you for entrusting me with this beautiful gift.

Paul, my husband. You have loved me as Christ loves the church. Thank you.

Samuel and Katelyn, my children. You have taught me to love boundlessly, forgive quickly and laugh out loud. You are my pure joy.

Preface

God speaks

The idea that we can hear God speak may seem presumptuous, but throughout the Bible we see God interacting with humanity. If we quiet our racing thoughts and be still for a moment, we can hear him. He is speaking all the time. God speaks through creation, the words and actions of people, everyday circumstances, our dreams and through his word.

We can also hear God when we ask him to speak, then write what we sense he is saying. I was in my teens when I first started journaling with God. I'd write a letter to him and ask what he'd like to say to me and I'd write down whatever came to mind. I'd imagine how God would start a letter to me, his child. Then, I'd draw on all the things I'd read in the Bible about how God sees humanity and what he thinks of his children, how he loves and cares for us, how he has forgiven us and cleansed us, how he has good plans for us, plans to give us a hope and a future. As my thoughts flowed from what I'd read and heard and had been taught about God, I would occasionally catch a glimpse of something new. I'd write a sentence that seemed completely fresh and I'd get excited as I realized perhaps that really was a moment when God spoke to me. I've journaled on and off over the years and have always found it to be an exercise that deepens my walk with him.

At the start of Lent 2020, I felt prompted to write a letter from God every day for forty days. Within weeks, all radio staff from United Christian Broadcasters, where I host a daily radio show, were required to go into self-isolation because one of our studio guests tested positive for Covid-19. I therefore found myself starting this daily letter from God just as the coronavirus was taking hold across much of Europe. Through all the panic, uncertainty and fear, the one thing I looked forward to most was being still at the start of the day and listening for what God wanted to say to me. Although this was a letter from God to me, these words carry timeless truths from the Bible and, as you read them, I hope they will encourage you as they did me. God bless you as you read this letter from your heavenly Father.

Day 1

My ways are not your ways. My thoughts are not your thoughts.

I am working all things together for your good as you remain in me and keep in step with me. Be still and know me directing and leading you, and you will see things you were not expecting. You will experience a harvest you had not considered as you worship me and seek me first. Consecrate yourself to me; strip back and lay aside all that weighs you down and threatens to distract you from my call on you. Cast your cares on me and I will care for you. Lean not on your own understanding, but trust in me and I will direct you and show you great and mighty things. Step out in faith and without fear.

Seek me with all your heart. Let not your heart be troubled. Don't become disheartened, but look to me to help you and uphold you. Let my joy be your strength. Put your hope and your expectation for deliverance in me.

I am your peace. I am your hope. I am your Deliverer.

Trust me. Hope in me.

Seek me. Love me.

I love you with an everlasting love.

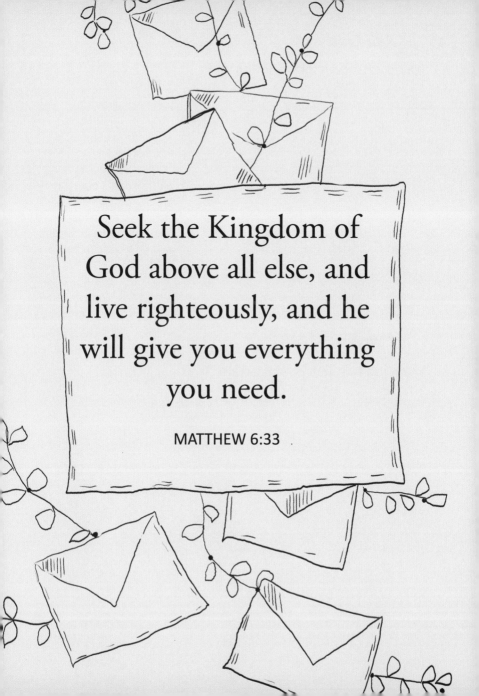

Seek the Kingdom of God above all else, and live righteously, and he will give you everything you need.

MATTHEW 6:33

Ask God

What does my heart seek more than you?

Prayer

Let my heart's longing be for you alone, my Lord.

My Thoughts

Day 2

Look up, child. Lift your head and rejoice.

I am your I Am. You are my child and I love you. Let hope rise, my beloved. Sing, weary soul. Rejoice in my salvation. Cast your cares, worries and anxieties onto me. Fear no more, for I am your protector. I am your Rock. Place your feet firmly on my truth. Build your life on me, then you will not be moved.

Though you sink into the muck and the mire, I will lift you up and place you on a firm foundation. Look to me, your hope, your anchor, your great Redeemer. Seek me with all your heart and I will be found by you and you will be found in me.

Be still and know me and the power of my salvation working in you and through you. Be encouraged. Be of good cheer, my beloved.

To the weak and weary sinner, I say, 'Look up.' I am your Rock, your salvation, your glory and the lifter of your head.

My grace is sufficient for you. My strength is made perfect in your weakness.

Be still, my child. Peace; be still, racing thoughts and anxious heart.

Rest in me.

He alone is my rock
and my salvation, my
fortress where I will
never be shaken.

PSALM 62:2

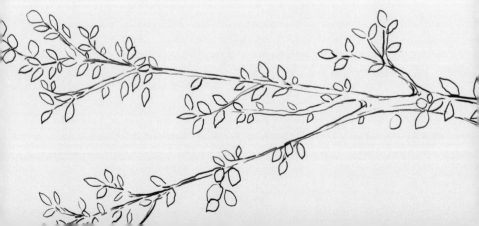

Ask God

In what area do I feel shaken and where have I lost hope?

Prayer

I look to you, Lord, to make me strong.

My Thoughts

Day 3

Beloved, my arm is not too short that it cannot reach you.

As I cup your face in the palms of my hand, lift up your gaze to mine. Look full in my face, and let the cares of this world fade. In the sinking depths of despair, look up and I will catch you. In the midst of deep troubles, and the shadow of the deep, there I will rescue you.

I am your enduring hope. You are my delight and I love you. Put your trust in me. Seek me with all your heart and I will be found by you. I will strengthen and sustain you.

Keep your eyes on me. Look to me. I am the author and finisher of your faith. Let not your heart be troubled. You are my precious one. Receive my love. Live in my love.

Turn to me, child, and allow the splendour of my gaze to touch your face. Let strength rise. Let hope be renewed. Let fear fade. Be restored. You shall live and not die. My light has risen on you this day.

Go in my name and in my power.

You are mine. I have redeemed you.

Listen! The LORD's arm is not too weak to save you, nor is his ear too deaf to hear you call.

ISAIAH 59:1

Ask God

When have I felt out of your reach, my Lord?

Prayer

Remind me, God, to lift my gaze to you when I am tempted to let my head fall in despair.

My Thoughts

Day 4

Swing wide heaven's gates and let blessing rain down. Open heaven's doors and flood the earth with favour.

Look to me with expectancy and know my abundant provision. Press in to me. Lean in and hear my voice. Draw close and I will take you on an adventure you cannot yet comprehend. This is the adventure of a life with me. Step out in faith and see my favour follow. I am leading you in the way everlasting. Follow me.

Cast your bread upon the waters. Look up. Look ahead. Sow good seed in good soil and run with me. I will bring the harvest. A bountiful blessing will come.

Look to me, walk with me, hear my voice, talk with me and let me lead you. Feel your burdens lighten and watch your cares fall by the wayside. Now, take up your cross and follow me. Run with me. Trust me to keep you going. Hope in me and I will give you the strength you need.

My joy wakes you from your slumber and propels you forward. Incline your ear to me. Hear me. Come away with me, my love.

With me, you can faithfully finish this race.

Open for me the
gates of the righteous;
I will enter and
give thanks to the LORD.
This is the gate
of the LORD through which
the righteous may enter.
I will give you thanks,
for you answered me;
you have become my
salvation.

PSALM 118:19–21 (NIV)

Ask God

What's keeping me from entering your presence?

Prayer

You are good, God, and I come into your presence with thanksgiving.

My Thoughts

Day 5

I love you. Nothing can separate you from my love. Not the giddy heights of great success, nor the depths of deep despair, when your hopes are all but dashed.

Nothing and no one can snatch you from my hand. You are mine and I love you. I delight in you. I remain faithful, even when you lose faith. I pursue you with an everlasting love. Where can you go from my presence? I am here. Always.

Be still, racing thoughts. Quiet, anxious heart. Know your Maker, cold, hard heart.

Turn your face to me. I will take your heart of stone and give you a heart of flesh. Though you fall a thousand times, I will forgive you and cleanse you, and you will rise. Like waves of the ocean cleanse the earth, so my love will wash over you and cleanse you. You are my righteousness. My holy and anointed one. Rise, my love, and walk free. You are delivered. You cannot outrun my love.

Be still. Be at peace. Let my love cover you.

Rest in me. Be free from fear.

Know my love. I have ransomed you. I am your great Redeemer.

You are my beloved.

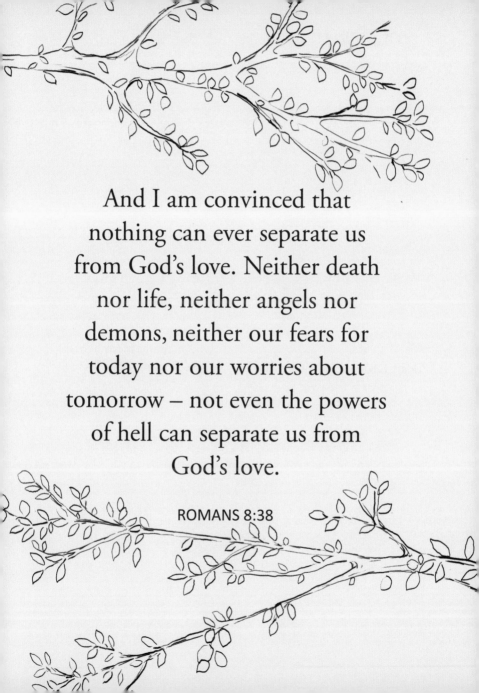

And I am convinced that
nothing can ever separate us
from God's love. Neither death
nor life, neither angels nor
demons, neither our fears for
today nor our worries about
tomorrow – not even the powers
of hell can separate us from
God's love.

ROMANS 8:38

Ask God

Why do I struggle to receive your love?

Prayer

Thank you, God, that nothing can separate me from your love.

My Thoughts

Day 6

Wake up, my love.

When you go to sleep, I am with you. When you rise, I am by your side. I will never leave you.

As the sun rises in the east, so is my faithful and abiding love for you. Breathe in deep and know me. Let hope rise. Lift up your eyes to the horizon. Let your vision extend. Joy comes this morning. I've woken you up. Hello, my love. I made this day for you. Keep in step with me. Talk with me. Quiet yourself, that you may hear me.

Look at the birds of the air. They sing my praises throughout the day. They don't worry or fear. They don't become anxious or distressed. They trust me. I've got you. I'm holding you. I have written your name on the palm of my hand. You are in my heart, my beloved.

Look to me. I am your Provider. I am your Comforter. Look and see all that I have for you. Look at the fields, they are ripe with a harvest. Come, join me. Let's bring in the harvest. I have equipped you with all you need. I will sustain you.

You are my love.

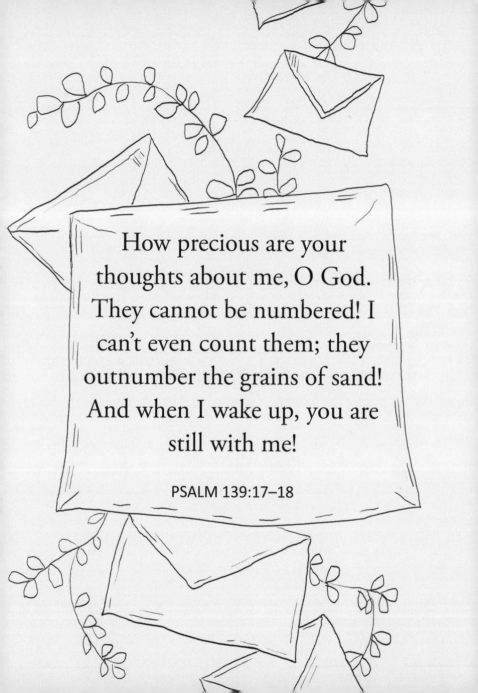

How precious are your thoughts about me, O God. They cannot be numbered! I can't even count them; they outnumber the grains of sand! And when I wake up, you are still with me!

PSALM 139:17–18

 ## *Ask God*

What do you want me to do today?

 ## *Prayer*

Let me be aware of your leading, and help me follow.

My Thoughts

Day 7

Come away with me, my love. Drink my living water and be filled.

Let not your heart be troubled. Believe in me. Live through me. My strength is made perfect in your weakness. Bring your weakness, your burdens, your weariness, anxieties, fears and troubles, and place them all at my feet.

I will sustain you and uphold you with my righteous right hand. Do not fear or be anxious about anything.

Come, rest here awhile. Take my yoke upon you. Let the lightness of my burden rest on you. Take up your cross and follow me. My joy is your strength. Draw near to me.

Be still and know me. My peace is yours. I love you.

Delight in me. Let strength rise as you take your fill of me. You are my beloved.

I delight in you. Trust me. I've got you. Rest secure in the palm of my hand. You will not be shaken, though the earth be moved. You will not be destroyed, though the mountains fall. Stretch out your hand. I've got you. I'm holding you. Peace. Be still. Rest here awhile. Delight in me and find rest for your soul.

You are mine.

But those who drink the
water I give will never be
thirsty again. It becomes
a fresh, bubbling spring
within them, giving them
eternal life.

JOHN 4:14

Ask God

What areas of my life are dry?

Prayer

Lord, I need your life-giving water. Fill me afresh and help me to delight in you alone.

My Thoughts

Day 8

Your praise clears away the dark clouds and lets the sunshine in. Sing, barren one. You thought you were without hope and a future, but from the depths, you rise. In the darkness, you sing. From the pit, you shout aloud.

Rise, my love. Come up here for a while. Look at the view. This is your life in focus. My perspective on you in your world. Come out of the shadows and into the light. Wow! You are beautiful.

Put your hand in mine and walk this way. We went through that cold, dark valley together and I never left you, but now it's time to walk up here in the sunlight. The lessons you learnt in the valley, you carry with you up here on the high hills. And I'm still with you.

I love this adventure with you. Let's go this way.

My song is in you. My heart overflows with love for you.

Let's stop here for a moment. Can you feel it? Just breathe. Let all your fears flow out and breathe me in. I am your peace. I am your confidence. I am your joy. I am your hope. I Am.

I love you.

In my distress I called to the LORD, and he answered me. From deep in the realm of the dead I called for help, and you listened to my cry.

JONAH 2:2 (NIV)

 *Ask God*

In what areas have I chosen to remain hidden and in the dark?

 *Prayer*

From the depths of my deep despair I rise and sing to you.

My Thoughts

Day 9

See, the clouds have cleared. The sun is breaking through. Mourning has turned to dancing and sorrow to joy. Strength rises. Hope is renewed. The weary traveller rejoices. What was lost, is now found. What was dead, now lives.

Speak of my glory and goodness. My kindness is life to you. My song is in you. Turn your ear to me and hear my still, small voice.

In faith, follow me. Lean on me and trust in me. Though it seems scary, step out and, in an instant, you'll know I'm here with you. Always.

I provide for all you need. Look for me, and you will find me. Even in the noise and clutter of your racing thoughts, in the midst of your shame and dismay, I will break through and you will hear me clearly. My child, I have loved you with an everlasting love. Nothing can separate you from my love. No one can keep you from my love. I am your Abba God, your heavenly Father who will never abandon you. I am your Good Shepherd.

Incline your ear to me. I am directing you, leading you, tenderly and lovingly showing you the way.

Follow me.

Come to me with your ears wide open. Listen, and you will find life.

ISAIAH 55:3

 *Ask God*

My God, reveal the source of my racing, noisy thoughts.

 *Prayer*

Speak, Lord, I am listening.

My Thoughts

Day 10

When your heart faints, I will sustain you. When you think you've failed, know that, in me, you are victorious. Let the voices of doubt and despair be stilled. Hear only my voice. I am with you even until the end of the ages.

The way. The truth. The life.

Come to me and know my peace. When the things of the world press in to steal your joy, I will be the lifter of your head.

I am your shield and your Protector. Your feet are fitted with my word and your life is hidden in me. Your foundation and your stronghold are found in me. I am your watchtower.

The enemy you thought would overwhelm you has faded to nothing, for I am your God, the One who loves you, so that nothing can overcome you.

You are mine. My beloved. No evil will befall you. I've got you. Nothing is too hard for you. I am your strength. No shadow will overtake you. I am your light. No wickedness will consume you. My goodness is in you and flowing through you.

You are my child. My precious possession. I love you and I will not let you go.

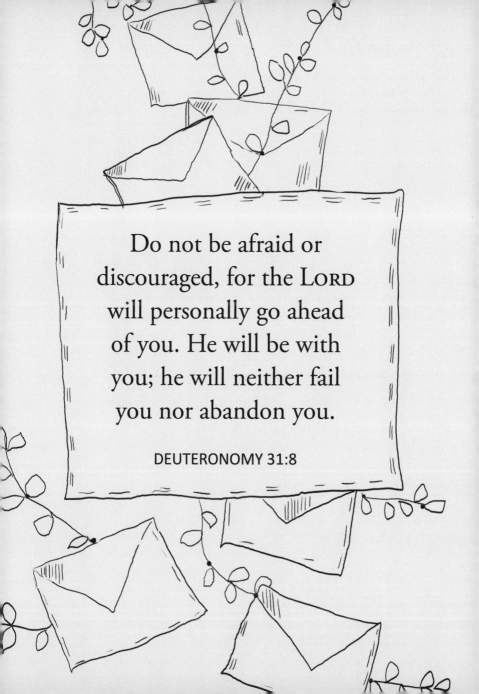

Do not be afraid or discouraged, for the LORD will personally go ahead of you. He will be with you; he will neither fail you nor abandon you.

DEUTERONOMY 31:8

Ask God

What's threatening to steal my joy?

Prayer

Let me hear and respond only to your voice over my life.

My Thoughts

Day 11

Shine.

Let the whole world see that you are mine. A city on a hill cannot be hidden. Light in the dark. Salt in a flavourless space. I have called you. I have chosen you. Go, make disciples. Speak of me to your world.

Turn to me and hear my voice. This is my song of redemption. I'm singing it over you. You are my redeemed. I have bought you with my own life. The enemy of your soul no longer has a hold over you. You are free. Now walk as one who is free. Released from bondage, you are made whole.

Journey on with a lightness in your step. My smile is on you, my child. I am with you always. I have birthed you and I will not abandon you. I have fed you and cared for you. I have cleaned you, clothed and raised you. With loving-kindness, I have shown you a better way.

You have grown in my love. Your roots go down deep. Like the mighty oak, you are strong. You will not waver in your devotion to me. You will not falter or fall.

I have called you by name. You are mine.

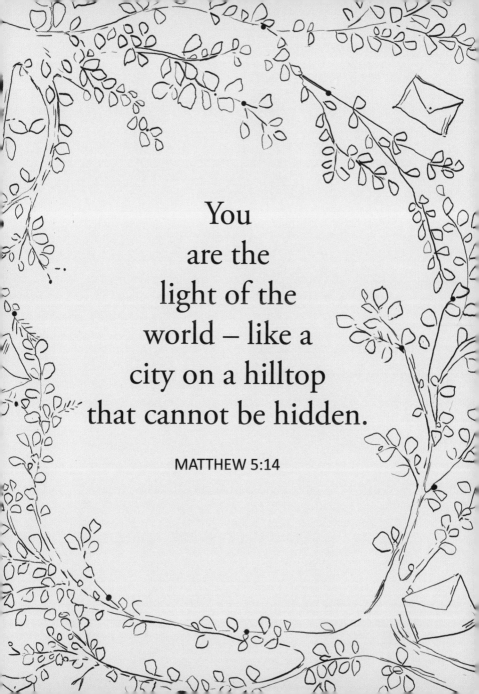

You
are the
light of the
world – like a
city on a hilltop
that cannot be hidden.

MATTHEW 5:14

Ask God

Who do you want me to disciple?

Prayer

Thank you, God, that I am yours.

My Thoughts

Day 12

Come up for air. Now breathe. You are alive, child. Now live.

See what I see? Touch my world as I have touched you. Devote yourself to my way and lead others to do the same. I've got you. Here, put your hand in mine. Look to me. Watch me. See, I've got you.

Shine, like the stars. Glow, like the embers stoked in a warm fire. Be who I created you to be, child. Live, love, move. In me. Through me. Sing. Lift up your voice, child. Beloved. Sing, weary soul. Sing. Lift up a mighty shout. From deep within. Let love flow. Healed, so you may heal. Touched, so you may touch. Restored, so you may restore. That's me. In you. Just be. Everlasting, unconditional, enduring love. Birthed, that you may birth. Bring forth life. Speak, child. Speak. Speak life. Live life. No turning back. Look ahead. Carry my load. Feel that? It's easy. No stress. No worry. No trouble. No fear. Just lightness. Abundant life. You've got what you need. Everything. I am your all. I am all you need. You've got this.

Journey on. Sojourn ahead. Lightness. Life. Love.

Peace. Be still. Rest.

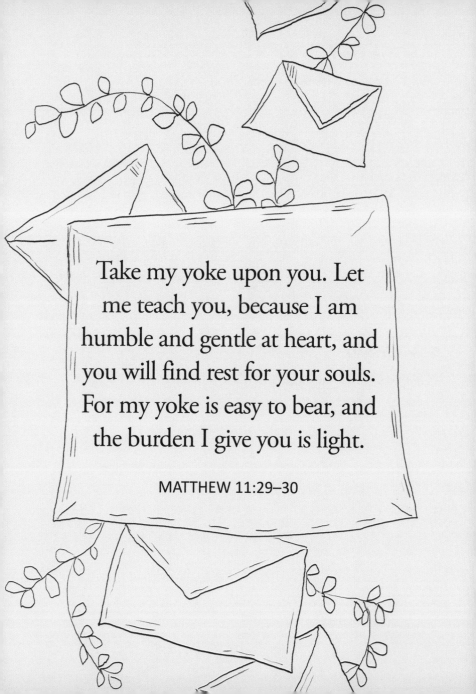

Take my yoke upon you. Let me teach you, because I am humble and gentle at heart, and you will find rest for your souls. For my yoke is easy to bear, and the burden I give you is light.

MATTHEW 11:29–30

Ask God

What do you want me to bear today?

Prayer

Lord, help me live from a place of rest.

My Thoughts

Day 13

Draw near to me, and I will draw near to you. I will show you great and mighty things.

I have cleansed you. You stand before me, clean. Don't bow your head, my child. You have nothing to fear. Look up, precious one. You are redeemed. Ransomed. Restored. Made whole. Newness of life is coursing through your veins. My life is at work in your life. Child, I love you.

Beloved, know me. Trust me. Lean on me. Still your soul and be at rest. Peace, be still.

Joy in me. Hope through me. Live and move by my power, made perfect in your weakness. Not by your own strength. How lovely you are, my beloved. How precious are your ways to me. I walk with you. I talk with you. Hear me. Listen. Incline your ear to hear me lead you.

I will never leave you. I will never forsake you. I have never left you. I have never forsaken you. Great is my faithfulness to you. I am your Rock and your strong foundation. Build on me. Be devoted to me alone.

I will sustain you. In all things and at all times.

I love you. Journey on.

His purpose was for the nations to seek after God and perhaps feel their way toward him and find him – though he is not far from any one of us. For in him we live and move and exist.

ACTS 17:27–28

Ask God

In what areas of my life am I relying on my own strength?

Prayer

Help me, Lord, to live in and through your power today.

My Thoughts

Day 14

Mighty one. Stand firm on this rock, that you may not be moved. Know my deliverance. My release. My saving grace.

Arise, shine, for your light has come. I am your glory and the lifter of your head.

Purity and holiness is what I long for, to find one who is just and kind and true. Where can I find a willing heart that beats for me? Who has clean hands and a pure heart?

You are my loved one. Come to me and find rest for your searching soul. The things you desire – the righteous way, the just words, the kind eyes, the loving hands, the joy bubbling up and the tender mercy – are yours. For you are mine and, in me, you have my heart. Live now, as one who is loved.

Rise, mighty one, in whom are the words of life. Speak with a boldness that comes from my throne. Let justice shine like the noonday sun, let tender mercy fall like soaking rain. Let comfort flow from your lips that all who hear might live to glorify my holy name. Righteousness and justice, mercy and loving-kindness are in you and come from you.

In my name. Go.

Who may climb the mountain
of the LORD? Who may stand
in his holy place? Only those
whose hands and hearts are
pure, who do not worship
idols and never tell lies.

PSALM 24:3–4

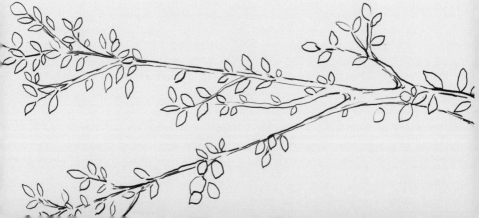

Ask God

What am I searching for?

Prayer

Teach me to live as one who is loved by the King of heaven.

My Thoughts

Day 15

Wake up, my love. See, deliverance is here. Hope rises. Remember the rainbow? The one that caught you off guard. Bold and bright on a day you did not expect it and in a place you were not searching for it. As quickly as it appeared, it was gone. You searched for it, but you could not find it. It was a reminder of my promise to you, though. My hope and my deliverance; yours for the taking. You need only step into the promise and live it. And what of that moon? Breaking through the dark clouds, shining through the heavy rain. You are my light. You are my hope for this dark world. I am your glory and the lifter of your head.

Lift up your voice of refreshing in the desert places. Declare my goodness in the valley of the shadow of death. Speak of my loving-kindness until the end of days. Know my salvation and speak of my glory. You are light. You are love.

Go, child. I am with you this day. Journey on. Seek my face, sing my praise, honour my way.

Speak and live. Light up the dark way. I love you always.

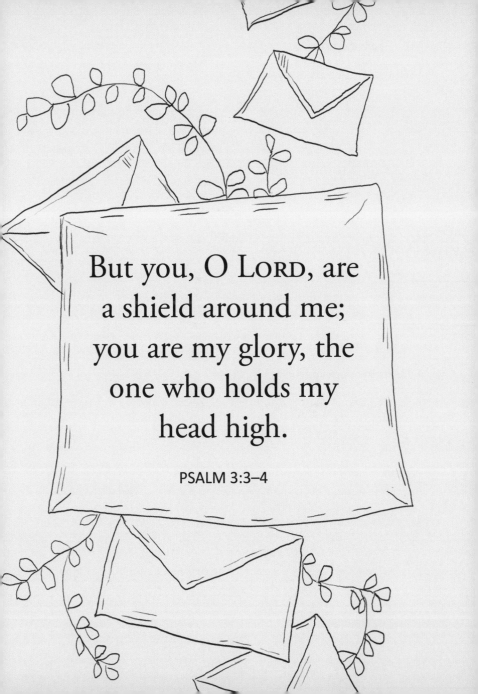

But you, O LORD, are
a shield around me;
you are my glory, the
one who holds my
head high.

PSALM 3:3–4

 *Ask God*

When did I rush by you, my Lord?

 *Prayer*

Help me to notice you today, Jesus.

My Thoughts

Day 16

Taste and see that I, the Lord, am good. I am good to all who walk in my way and trust in me. You will not be moved, though the earth give way and the mountains be thrown into the sea. You will stand and see my glory.

Watch, wait and pray.

Seek my face, turn from your sin and walk with me. Know me as I know you: far beyond the widest expanse and the deepest of seas, so great is my love for you. Never ending. Jump into my love and experience the most exciting adventure of your life.

No weapon formed against you shall prosper. Draw near to me and I will draw near to you. I will never let go of your hand.

Rest in me. Be still. Don't worry or become anxious. I've got you. I am strong to deliver and mighty to save. Though the enemy rise up against you, you will not be defeated for you are my child and I will never abandon you. You have been redeemed. Now live free. You are mine. I have not forgotten you.

Sing my love. Declare my goodness in this, the land of the living.

Taste and see that
the LORD is good.
Oh, the joys of
those who take
refuge in him!

PSALM 34:8

Ask God

Where am I living as one who is defeated?

Prayer

Thank you, God, that by your mighty power I have overcome.

My Thoughts

Day 17

Hope, in the midst of despair.

When the voice of fear and terror speaks, my voice speaks louder. Put your hope in me and let me be your joy. A pleasant song. I am a sweet aroma. My words are in your mouth, speaking life, love and truth. A voice crying out in the wilderness.

Remind my people to put their hope in me alone. You shall live and not die. Live to glorify my name throughout all the earth. Sing, though you are barren. You have found favour with the King. I am the Lord your God. Mighty in battle and rich to provide for all your needs. Holy and just.

Seek my face. Turn and walk in my way, that I may heal you. Know me as I know you. Be made whole, my child. In you are the words of life. I am your Rock and your Redeemer.

Strengthen my people. When their hearts faint and the earth succumbs to despair, turn hearts back to me.

Seek me in all you do. Learn from me and I will show you great and mighty things. Desire me and walk in my way and I will make you strong.

You will overcome.

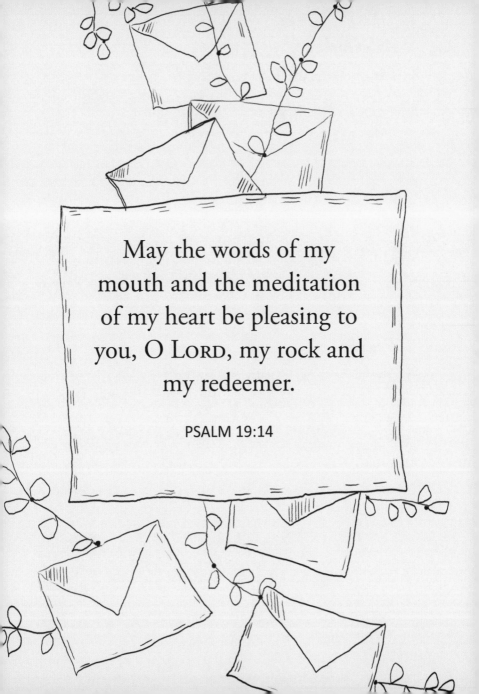

May the words of my mouth and the meditation of my heart be pleasing to you, O LORD, my rock and my redeemer.

PSALM 19:14

Ask God

Where am I in need of your healing power?

Prayer

Let your words be on my lips today, Lord my God.

My Thoughts

Day 18

Those who trust in the Lord do good. They live peacefully in the land. They have hope and do not despair.

This is your time, so be strong and courageous. Do not tremble or be afraid. Seek me only. Be still and know me. Trust in me alone. You are my redeemed child and I love you. Live as one who is loved by the Almighty; by the King of heaven, the Most High God.

Deliverance comes from me alone, your Rock and your Redeemer. Outside of me, you can do nothing.

Look, I am making a way in the wilderness. Streams in the desert. See, hope flows from my throne. Taste and see that I, the Lord, am good. Look to the mountains and your sight will fail. Look to the valleys and your heart will grow weary. Look to the rivers and you'll be overwhelmed. Outside of me, you can do nothing.

Look to me. I am your Rock. I am your Deliverer. I am your Redeemer. I am your Good Shepherd. I take good care of you. I have sought you out and found you.

I have brought you back to the fold, for you are mine.

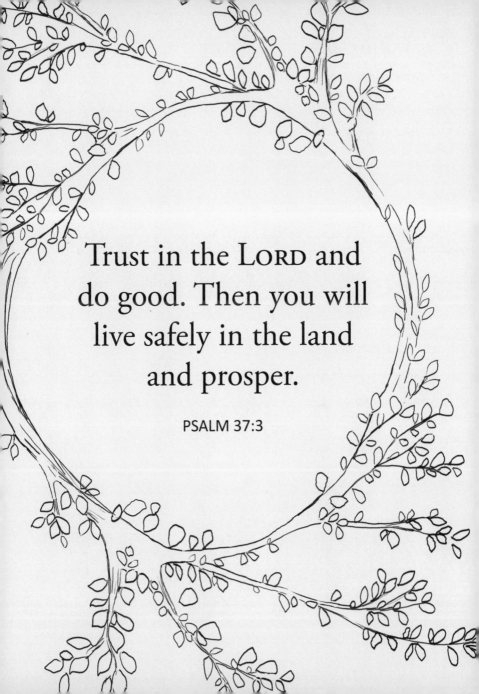

Trust in the LORD and
do good. Then you will
live safely in the land
and prosper.

PSALM 37:3

Ask God

Where do I lack peace?

Prayer

Let your peace be my peace.

My Thoughts

Day 19

Build up the broken. Speak truth with love. Live in my light, that those who wander in darkness may see and come, weary and worn, to me.

Shine my love. Live a life that glows. Let love lead. Let hope bolster. Let my Spirit guide. Journey on.

Freedom is your song. Awake, O sleeper. Stir in the morning light. You are my delight. See, I am here with you always.

Step out in boldness. Let courage rise. Go. By faith. Walk with me. Talk with me. Speak through me and turn from all that threatens to weigh you down and draw you back. Set your face like flint on the path I have set out for you. My child. My delight. My precious one. You are mine and I love you. Clothed in righteousness. Speak of my faithfulness.

Your children rise and call you blessed. My favour is on you. Let it flow through you. Be still and know me. See what I am about to do through you. Humble yourself and I will lift you up. Climb the mountain of the Lord and know my presence and my peace.

Sing, for your salvation has come. I am your Deliverer.

Some of you will rebuild the deserted ruins of your cities. Then you will be known as a rebuilder of walls and a restorer of homes.

ISAIAH 58:12

Ask God

Where do you want me to rebuild?

Prayer

Let your love lead me today.

My Thoughts

Day 20

Out of the ashes, you rise. Out of the dust, you breathe life. Sing and rejoice. I am the Lord, your Maker.

Rise, my love, your enemy is gone. The one who tormented you has fled and you are free. Free to walk with me. Free of the burden of sin that entangled you and kept you bound to a life of slavery. In me and by my strength, you walk with your head held high.

By my power, you are made perfect. Your weakness has been made strong. My thoughts are becoming your thoughts. My ways, your ways. You are mine. My precious one. My delight and my glory. My Spirit is in you. You have all you need. I am a salve to your wounds and you will bring healing to your world through me.

Turn to me and look in my face. Remain in me. Let my words remain in you and flow through you. Receive from me all you need.

Be salt and light. Life and love. Child of my loins. Heart of my heart. Step out into all that I have for you.

I am with you, my love, even until the end of the age.

To all who mourn in Israel, he will give a crown of beauty for ashes, a joyous blessing instead of mourning, festive praise instead of despair. In their righteousness, they will be like great oaks that the LORD has planted for his own glory.

ISAIAH 61:3

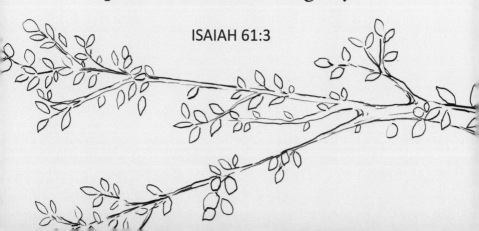

 *Ask God*

What pain am I still clinging to?

 *Prayer*

As you have healed me, let me bring healing.

My Thoughts

Day 21

Awake, my love. Rise from your slumber. Shine, for your light has come and my glory is on you.

Let the people hear of my faithfulness throughout all generations. I am the Lord, the Holy One, and my word is in your mouth. How lovely are your feet, my child, as you carry my word. How sweet on your lips, my beloved. Like honey to those who are perishing. Speak life, my child. Fear not. I am with you. Go boldly for I am your God. I am your Rock and your Redeemer, and I will sustain you. As I have through all your days, so will I uphold you and carry you. I will journey with you.

Though the earth be shaken and the hearts of people faint, you will remain firm in faith. You will not be moved. For my word is in you and flows from you. It is your firm foundation. Stand on my word. Speak my love.

From the overflow of your heart, let my heart touch humanity. Call out. Sound the alarm. Let my people awake.

Rise up. Your enemy is scattered and you have the victory.

In me, you have life. Now live.

How beautiful on the
mountains are the feet
of the messenger who
brings good news, the
good news of peace and
salvation, the news that
the God of Israel reigns!

ISAIAH 52:7

Ask God

Remind me, Lord, of the times you have strengthened me.

Prayer

Help me share the hope I have found in you, my God.

My Thoughts

Day 22

Those who walk with the wise, will be wise. Those who sit with fools, will themselves become foolish.

Choose this day whom you will serve.

Follow me and I will show you the right path. It will be a difficult and treacherous path at times. It is a narrow and harrowing way for sure, darkness and storms for the most part. But oh, the joy, precious one, the joy of following in its way. This path leads to salvation; it works in you the most good. It leads to righteousness, and justice is in its steps. Tread lightly in some parts, run earnestly and with diligence in other parts, trudge forward through the muck and the mire from time to time, and walk lightly with the sunlight in your face at times.

Walk with me. Stay close. I'll lead you. Can you see me? Just one step ahead. Look for me. Here I am. Close. Keep walking. Keep moving. And if you need to rest a while, rest, but stay on this path. It leads to life.

Journey on, Christian soldier. Pilgrim through this barren land. My strength is in you and flowing through you.

I've got you. Journey on.

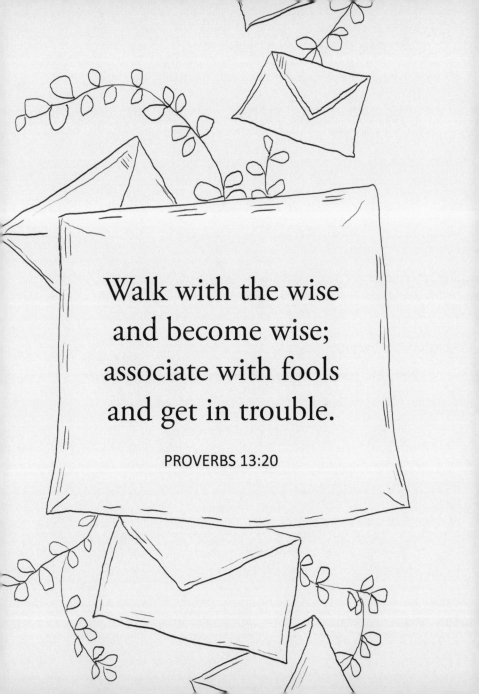

Walk with the wise
and become wise;
associate with fools
and get in trouble.

PROVERBS 13:20

Ask God

What good are you working in me on this part of the journey?

Prayer

When I am tempted to wander from this narrow path, steady me.

My Thoughts

Day 23

To the pure in heart, I show myself faithful. To the weak, I show myself strong. To the weary, I am mighty. To the merciful, I am mercy. To the generous, I am more than enough. Stretch out your hand in love and find me, full of love. In your kindness, you will know me kind. Work for peace and know my peace with you. Let hope rise. Fear is vanquished and courage rises. In meekness and gentleness, you will gain all you need for I am your Provider. My love is upon you and flowing in and through you.

The way. The truth. The life. Light of the world. Salt to a flavourless world.

My strength is made perfect in your weakness. From generation to generation my favour flows. Beautiful and bright, my delight and joy.

I am forever faithful. Trustworthy. True. I love you.

Be holy as I am holy. Be righteous as I am righteous.

My power is made perfect in weakness. You are made new. Live new. The old doesn't fit you anymore. Live free. A slave to righteousness, holiness and purity, yet free of the bondage of sin and death. Your chains are gone.

Forever free.

I know the LORD is
always with me. I
will not be shaken,
for he is right
beside me.

PSALM 16:8

Ask God

Where do I feel weak?

Prayer

Help me lean on you today, my Lord.

My Thoughts

Day 24

In your faithfulness, I show myself faithful. Your justice shines like the noonday sun. You will not be crushed.

Though the earth be moved and the mountains give way, though the seas surge and bring ruin to the coastline, do not fear. I am your Rock and your Redeemer. Hope in me. I am your forever foundation. Build your life on me. Keep your eyes on me. Look to me, your Maker, your source. Allow your roots to go deep in me. I am your I Am.

Though the earth is ravaged by pestilence and plague, you will remain free from the terror, for I have commanded my angels to shield and protect you. You will remain fruitful in this season of lack.

I am your God. You will not falter or fail. You will not grow faint or lose heart, for I am your strong Deliverer. Look to me, your help in time of need.

My delight and joy, that's you. Beautiful one, my peace is your peace. My grace is enough for you. My power is made perfect in weakness.

When you feel weary, look to me and find strength. I am enough.

I'm holding you, my child.

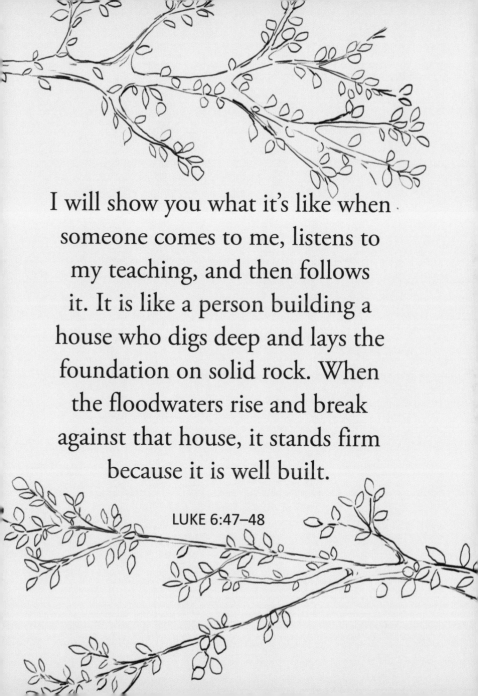

I will show you what it's like when someone comes to me, listens to my teaching, and then follows it. It is like a person building a house who digs deep and lays the foundation on solid rock. When the floodwaters rise and break against that house, it stands firm because it is well built.

LUKE 6:47–48

 *Ask God*

Where am I in danger of building on sinking sand?

 *Prayer*

Let me be still, so I can hear your voice and follow you.

My Thoughts

Day 25

Comfort my people, comfort. Exhort my chosen, exhort.

To the weak and weary, I am strength. Nourish and nurture my children as I have nurtured you. I am your Good Shepherd and, as I lead you, lead. Sing and let your restless soul be at peace. Come walk with me, my love. Come close and know me. In me, you find rest. Through me, you are able to scale the high mountain, overcome the raging sea and live through the fire. You will not suffer loss.

My guardian angels are by your side. I am your Defender. Your strong tower. Your mighty God. Run to me. Draw near to me in stillness and know me. My shadow shields you from the blazing sun. In the cleft of the rock, you will find rest. Under my wings, I will protect you. Humble yourself before me and I will lift you up.

Look to me, I am your Rock and your Redeemer; your strong and mighty Deliverer. Mighty in battle. Victorious in all things.

Set your face like flint in the direction I am leading you and, as you do, joy will come. Journey on.

My strength is in you. Journey on.

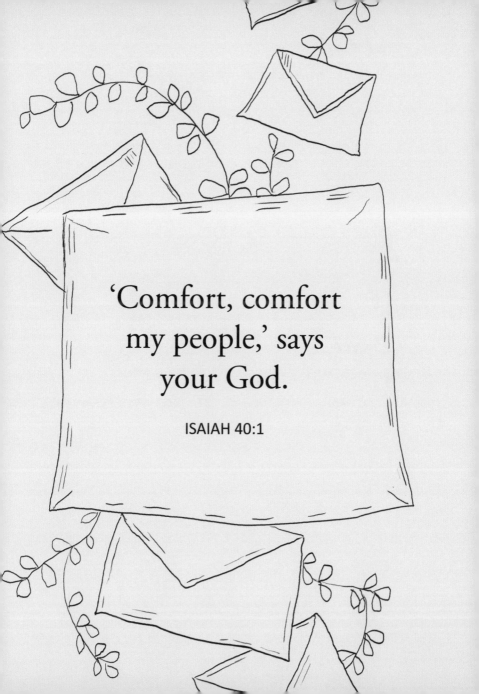

'Comfort, comfort
my people,' says
your God.

ISAIAH 40:1

Ask God

Where is the cleft in the rock; that I may rest in you?

Prayer

I humble myself before you, Lord. As you lead, I will follow.

My Thoughts

Day 26

Prepare the way, prepare the way for my people to walk in it. Make straight the paths, make straight the paths as I lead you. Journey on. I'll lead you.

Walk this way, my child, come follow me. This is the way, walk in it. Do not look to the side, keep your eyes straight ahead. Walk with me. Here, take my hand. Do not fear.

I am generous and good and my way leads to life. Abundant life. Full, joyful, exuberant life.

Teach my people what I have taught you, that they may know my way, that they may not be found wanting. Learn from me and I will show you what to say. My words are in your mouth, my child. Speak as you hear my word. Point out the way as I lead you. Trust me. Lean on me. Learn from me and follow me. Stay right here, by my side. Look to me and you won't wander far. Keep your eyes fixed on me. I Am. The author and finisher of your faith.

What I started in you, I am continuing. Until I see you face to face.

Well done, good and faithful servant. Walk on.

Listen! It's the voice of someone shouting, 'Clear the way through the wilderness for the Lord! Make a straight highway through the wasteland for our God!'

ISAIAH 40:3

Ask God

Where is the rough, uneven ground that you want me to prepare for you?

Prayer

God, show me what you want me to say today.

My Thoughts

Day 27

My beloved. You are being made perfect. Into my likeness.

Look to me. Walk with me. Through the fiery trials, you will not be burned. In the midst of the dark valley, you will know my light. I am leading you. I am showing you the way. In quietness and rest, you will know me. My peace.

I am your hope. When you look for me, I will be found by you. Moments of delight and wonder. You will find them, when you look for me. When you seek me with all your heart.

Quiet your racing thoughts. What do you hear? Still your anxious mind. What do you see? In restlessness, quiet your soul and find stillness in me.

I love you. Can you feel it? I love you. Can you hear it? You are my beloved and I love you. I am awakening your soul to love. To my love. Everlasting. As far as the East is from the West. As vast as the deep of the ocean. As high as the heavens.

As I have loved you, love others. Speak. Show. Be love. Perfect love casts out fear. I am perfect love. I Am.

I love you.

'In those days
when you pray,
I will listen.
If you look for me
wholeheartedly,
you will find me.
I will be found by you,'
says the LORD.

JEREMIAH 29:12–14

Ask God

What does my heart seek in the midst of the fiery trial?

Prayer

Help me see the moments of delight and wonder you provide.

My Thoughts

_____

_____

_____

_____

_____

_____

_____

_____

_____

_____

_____

_____

_____

_____

Day 28

To your troubled heart, I speak peace. To your weary soul, I speak strength. To fear, faith. To lack, provision.

I am all you need. Your Maker, Creator, Father and Friend, your Saviour and Redeemer. Mighty in power, rich in love, full of grace and abundant in mercy. Forgiving your sin. Your wayward and rebellious heart. Your wandering will and faithlessness. Even there I will find you and restore you. My faithfulness to you extends from generation to generation.

My wisdom is in you. When you seek wise counsel, you will find it in me. Lean not on your own understanding. My ways are not your ways, nor are my thoughts your thoughts. Seek me first and my kingdom. Learn from me. Seek to be holy as I am holy. Righteous, as I am righteous.

You can do all things through me. You are strong in me. Trust me with all your heart.

I love you, my beautiful one. Made perfect. My love. I am yours and you are mine.

In me you will find your sustenance. In me you will find rest.

I am bringing you into a spacious place. Rest here awhile and be at peace.

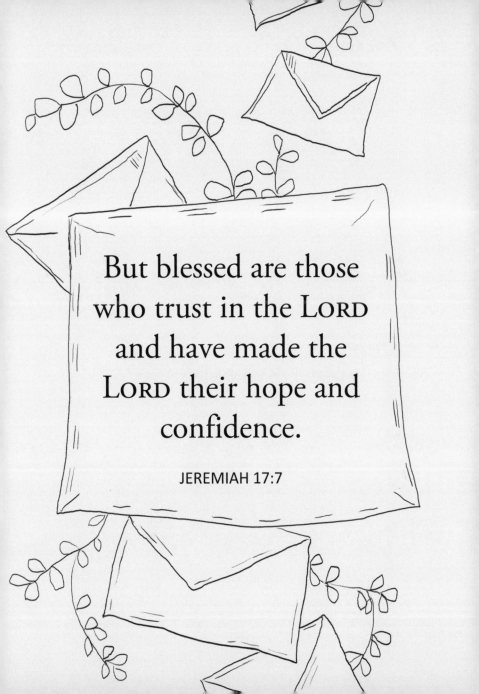

But blessed are those who trust in the LORD and have made the LORD their hope and confidence.

JEREMIAH 17:7

Ask God

Where have I wandered from you, my God?

Prayer

Forgive me, Lord. Lead me and help me follow you today.

My Thoughts

Day 29

As certain as the rising sun, so certain is my love for you morning by morning.

As bright as the moon on a clear night sky; though but a sliver, you see it. Light piercing through the dark. This is like my faithfulness to you, my precious one. My delight.

As vast as the heavens that stretch out before you as far as the eye can see, so are my care and compassion for you. Not one star is out of place. I see all. I know all. And I love you completely.

In the midst of the wonder of the world, I choose you. Bring your weary, dusty feet here, my beloved. Let me wash them. How beautiful are your feet as you carry the good news of my love.

Declare my faithfulness. My words are on your lips. Speak. The faithful love you have known, share it. Declare boldly and with great courage that my grace is sufficient. My power is made perfect in weakness. No one is too far gone. To the weary, I am strong. To the weak, I am mighty. I deliver those who are trapped in darkness.

I am your light, your strong tower.

For your unfailing love
is as high as the heavens.
Your faithfulness reaches
to the clouds.

PSALM 57:10

Ask God

In what ways have you shown me your love and faithfulness?

Prayer

Teach me to come to you in my strength and my weakness.

My Thoughts

Day 30

This load is not too heavy. This burden will not weigh you down. Take up your cross. Now, follow me. Not that load and burden. Don't allow yourself to be weighed down by the cares of the world. This yoke here is for you. I've given you all you need to carry this. Your care, worry and anxiety – those things all belong to me. Bring them here. Place them at my feet.

Here, yoke yourself to me, so we can walk side by side. Refuse to become a slave to the things that weigh you down and make you weary. My load is easy and my burden is light. I know you don't want to take up your cross, but it's the only way you can be my true disciple. It may look frightening and cumbersome, but it was made for you and with my help it will become a joy to bear.

In your journey with the cross, you will find a joy and a peace you cannot find anywhere else. My grace is sufficient for you. My power is made perfect in your weakness. We can do this together.

I will never leave you.

I am with you always.

Then Jesus said, 'Come to me, all of you who are weary and carry heavy burdens, and I will give you rest. Take my yoke upon you. Let me teach you, because I am humble and gentle at heart, and you will find rest for your souls. For my yoke is easy to bear, and the burden I give you is light.'

MATTHEW 11:28–30

Ask God

What do I need to lay at your feet?

Prayer

I take up my cross and follow you, Lord Jesus. I want to be your true disciple.

My Thoughts

Day 31

I have made you rich in love. You are strong in battle. Mighty in weakness. My compassion is in you and flowing from you.

Go in courage. Go in power. Victory is yours. Put on the full armour.

Your thoughts become my thoughts as you put on the helmet of salvation. I have replaced your heart of stone with a heart of flesh as you secure the breastplate of righteousness. Here, take the shield of faith so you can stand against the fiery darts of the enemy. My word is your sword and you can wield it as the Spirit teaches you. I am your belt of truth. It's central to all that you are. The shoes of the gospel of peace have been made to fit you perfectly.

I will teach you to pray. I'll remind you. Your fight is not against flesh and blood. You will make war, in my strength, against the principalities and powers of this dark age. You have the victory. Do not fear.

Go in my name. Victory is yours. Be bold and courageous. Do not tremble or be dismayed. The battle is mine. In me, you have won.

I am with you.

Always.

Put on the full armour of God, so that you can take your stand against the devil's schemes. For our struggle is not against flesh and blood, but against the rulers, against the authorities, against the powers of this dark world and against the spiritual forces of evil in the heavenly realms.

EPHESIANS 6:11–12 (NIV)

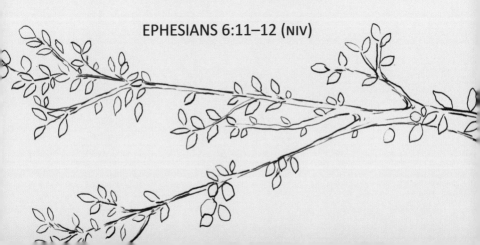

 ## *Ask God*

Where do I tremble and feel dismayed?

 ## *Prayer*

I put on the full armour you have given me that I may stand firm against the enemy. My hope is in you alone.

My Thoughts

Day 32

Clean hands and a pure heart are in you. I know you don't always see it, but I do. You think you are far from me, but you are near. You think your heart is hard, but it is soft and pure.

You are hidden in me. You live through me. I am perfect. Holy. Righteous. True. My Spirit is in you. You are becoming. In my presence, you are made right. Here with me, you are holy. So, live from a pure heart.

My love is in you, let it flow from you. Bring me your thoughts. They are becoming my thoughts. Learn from me. I'm leading you, my child. All that you need is in you. I have equipped you for such a time as this.

I am with you. Don't fear. My love is in you. My power. My self-control. Never will I leave you. Never will I forsake you.

My strength is made perfect in your weakness. Surrender to me. Lean on me and strength will rise. Hope becomes strong. Boldness and courage, grace and mercy bolster you. By my Spirit. All things are in you and flow from you.

Just be. For you are mine.

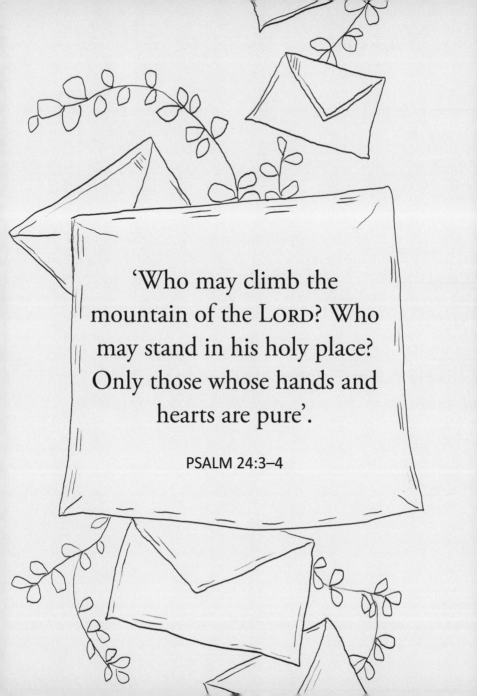

'Who may climb the mountain of the LORD? Who may stand in his holy place? Only those whose hands and hearts are pure'.

PSALM 24:3–4

Ask God

What resource do I have need of today?

Prayer

Help me see myself as you see me.

My Thoughts

Day 33

I've created a clean heart and renewed a right spirit within you.

I'll never cast you from my presence. My Spirit is within you.

I have restored to you the joy of your first love, now remain in my love. Let my words remain in you. This is how you bear much fruit.

With your roots deep down in me, you grow strong as I water you. As you study my word, truth feeds you. Nothing will shake you, my child, my beloved one. Your faith is firmly anchored in me. Your life is built on me. I am your solid Rock. Your firm foundation. I have not simply painted over the cracks of your life. I allowed you to be broken and have remade you. You are a new creation. Old things are gone. Your thinking, your actions, your words. Now live as new.

Forget the former things. Those things of old are no longer part of you. I have made a way in the wilderness. I am doing a new thing in you and through you.

Do not become weary. Take heart. Step out in faith.

I am with you always.

You are mine and I love you.

Create in me a clean heart, O God. Renew a loyal spirit within me.

PSALM 51:10

 *Ask God*

What 'old' thinking is threatening to pull me away from you?

 *Prayer*

Remind me of the joy of my first love.

My Thoughts

Day 34

To journey is one thing, but to journey with me and see as I see is pure delight. The adventure I had in mind for you all along. With ears unstopped, you hear my heart. With blinkers removed, you see as I see. The wonder of my plan. Out of my love comes life. Abundant life. The awkward, unbalanced, insecure steps of the small child become confident, strong and sure. You are my child and I love you. I've always loved you. I delight in you. My smile is on you. All that I am and all that I have is in you and flowing through you. Just be.

Sing, child. Beloved of the King. You are life and light and love. With your roots in me and your life firmly founded on me, you cannot falter. Journey with grace and in truth, by faith. Strong and secure. Immovable and with joy.

See your inheritance before you – souls. Hard hearts softened. Turned to me. Your prayers for the lost and for the saints have been heard. I have listened and answered.

I have turned my face towards you. Because I love you.

You are mine and I delight in you.

For,
'Who can know
the Lord's thoughts?
Who knows enough
to teach him?'
But we understand
these things,
for we have
the mind of Christ.

1 CORINTHIANS 2:16

Ask God

What are your thoughts towards me?

Prayer

Let me see as you see and hear as you hear.

My Thoughts

Day 35

Put your hope in me. I am the Lord.

Run to me. This is where you find rest for your troubled soul. Your broken walls are built up. Your weakness is made strong.

In me you live and move and have your being. To the depths of your guilt and shame, I speak forgiveness, deliverance and love. To despair, I speak hope. Rise, child, my thoughts are becoming your thoughts. Think on these things. My ways, your ways. Live like this. Mercy and justice are mine. In me, they are yours. With kindness and mercy my love touches you. Now reach out and touch with the same kindness, mercy, love and gentleness. My grace is all you need. My power is made perfect in your weakness.

Rise, my love. Do not be overcome with guilt and shame. Don't allow feelings of fear, doubt and despair to overwhelm you. My love reaches you. It's never-ending, never-failing.

I am faithful. My love for you is everlasting. As my love washes over you and heals you, so will you be a healing balm to all you encounter. To your children and your children's children.

Let your confidence be in me.

Rest in me.

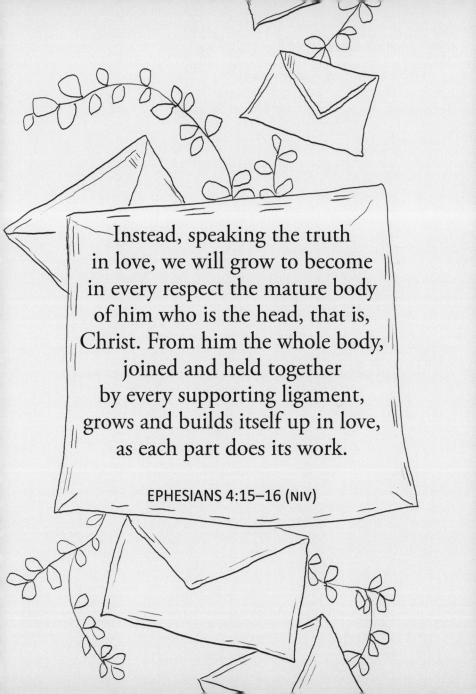

Instead, speaking the truth
in love, we will grow to become
in every respect the mature body
of him who is the head, that is,
Christ. From him the whole body,
joined and held together
by every supporting ligament,
grows and builds itself up in love,
as each part does its work.

EPHESIANS 4:15–16 (NIV)

Ask God

Where are the broken walls in my life?

Prayer

I place my confidence in you, Lord, for you are the Healer and Restorer.

My Thoughts

Day 36

Look back, my love. Take a moment and rest. What do you see?

Remember when you thought all was lost? Do you see me?

And the time you thought you wouldn't make it? I strengthened you. Look at courage rising. Lifting you.

And when you thought you lacked? I provided for your every need. In your hunger, I fed you. In your thirst, I refreshed you. In your fear, my love sustained you. I dried your tears and stilled your anxious thoughts. My peace calmed you in the midst of the raging storm. I lifted you from the miry pit. I placed your feet firmly on the rock. I led you through the darkest valley and brought you into the light. I made your brokenness whole. I spoke life to the places you thought were dead.

Where are you now, child? What do you need? Where do you lack? Whom do you fear? I am the same God who sustained you then. I am all you need now.

Remain in me. Let my words remain in you. Ask and it will be yours. Seek and you will find. Knock and the door will be opened to you.

Look to me.

The LORD your God, who is going before you, will fight for you, as he did for you in Egypt, before your very eyes, and in the wilderness. There you saw how the LORD your God carried you, as a father carries his son, all the way you went until you reached this place.

DEUTERONOMY 1:30–31 (NIV)

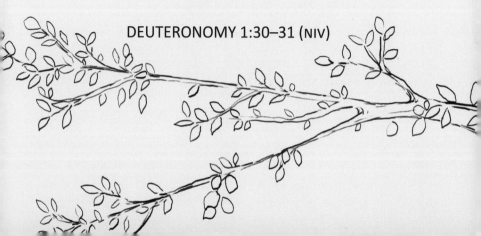

Ask God

Where have you cared for me?

Prayer

I bring all my cares and needs before you today. I lay them at your feet, my God.

My Thoughts

_____

_____

_____

_____

_____

_____

_____

_____

_____

_____

_____

_____

_____

_____

_____

_____

_____

_____

_____

Day 37

I am your Good Shepherd. I'll take care of you. When you wander far from this safe space, here near my heart, I'll go looking for you. When I see you from a distance, racked with guilt and shame, your heart broken and in tatters, I run to you, throw my arms around you, kiss you and welcome you home.

Remember who you are: my child. Nothing can change that. The moment you lift your eyes to me and begin to make your way back, in an instant you will be with me.

Your inheritance is secure. In my presence and through my power you become the truest version of you. That's why I came. So you can live fully alive.

Remain in me and let my words remain in you. Abide in me. Stay right here and learn from me. This is where you find rest.

My peace goes beyond anything you can comprehend. My grace is all you need. My power is perfect in weakness. Bring your failings to me. I'll make you strong. Rest here with me. I am your Protector and Provider.

I will never leave you. I won't abandon you. I am with you always.

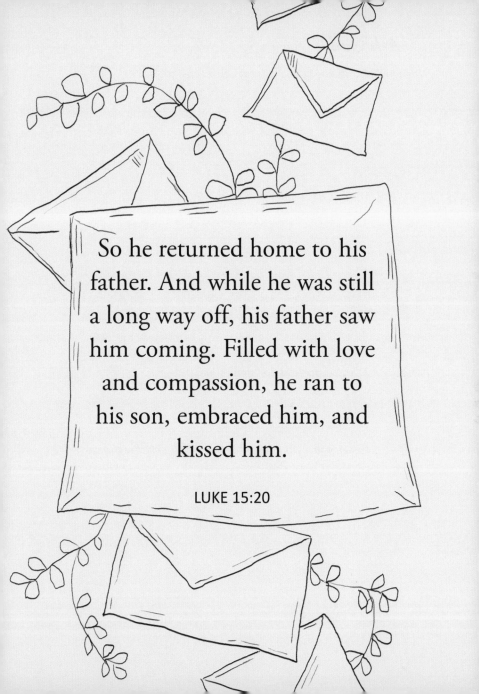

So he returned home to his father. And while he was still a long way off, his father saw him coming. Filled with love and compassion, he ran to his son, embraced him, and kissed him.

LUKE 15:20

Ask God

What guilt and shame keep me from being close to you?

Prayer

I lift my eyes to you, my Lord, remember me.

My Thoughts

Day 38

The desire of my heart is that you would know me, so stay close.

Walk with me. Talk with me. Hear from me. Be still. Rest. Stay close. From here you can see what I see. Hear what I hear. Know what I know. Look. Do you see? Wait here awhile and listen. Do you hear?

The mighty rise and fall. They triumph and then, suddenly, they stumble. I am the same yesterday, today, forever. I do not change. I will never leave you. I will not abandon you. With your hope and confidence in me, you will not be moved.

I cannot go against my word. It never fails. It will accomplish all I have spoken.

Trust in me. Lean on me. Hope in me. Have faith in me. You are my pure delight. This is your safe place. Have no fear. Only let faith rise. I am holding you. Here in my hand. In my presence you will know a joy that bubbles up from deep down. This is the kind of joy that will sustain you and carry you when you feel weak.

My peace is your peace.

Be at peace, child, and know my love.

Yahweh, your God, is among you, a mighty one who will save. He will rejoice over you with joy. He will calm you in his love. He will rejoice over you with singing.

ZEPHANIAH 3:17 (WEB)

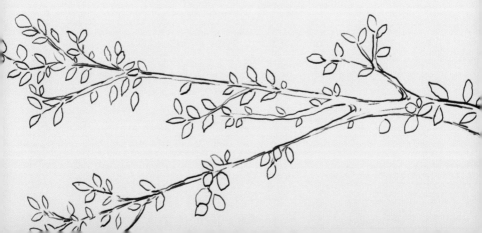

Ask God

What do you like about me?

Prayer

Let me like myself as you like me.

My Thoughts

Day 39

In the stillness you hear me. As you quiet yourself, you know I'm with you. It got noisy there for a while. It's difficult to hear me in the noise. Or see me in the busy crowd.

Here in this space. In this silence. When all is stripped away. This is where you get to hear me. See me. Know me. This is where you can draw near to me. Where you become the truest version of you. When it gets noisy again – and it will – remember this time. Reflect on this space. Consider the silence. You've got room to move.

Learn how to come back to this place. It's always been here. It'll be here when you seek it out. This is where you notice things you became too busy to see and hear things that bring deep joy. It's in this quiet that you find rest for your soul, in this stillness that you know me. It's here that you are led by my perfect peace. My strength sustains you as you become quiet.

This is only the start of the journey. We're only just beginning. Lean in and listen.

There's so much more to this great adventure.

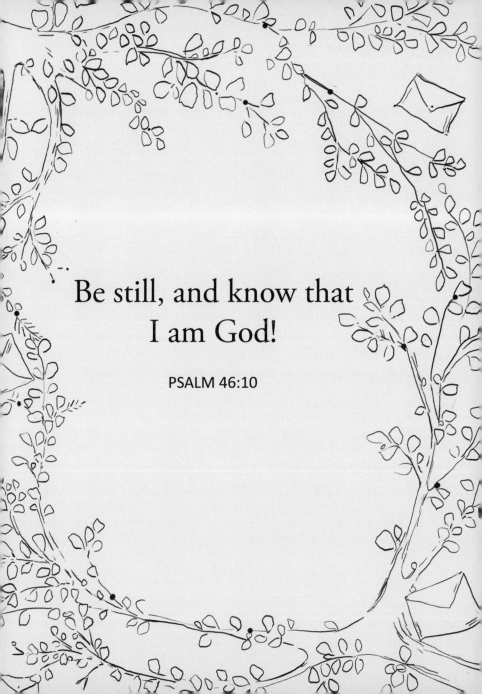

Be still, and know that
I am God!

PSALM 46:10

Ask God

Where is the noise in my life?

Prayer

Lead me to the quiet place where I can be still and hear you today.

My Thoughts

Day 40

Let not your heart be troubled. In weakness, say, 'I am strong.' In lack, declare, 'I am rich.' In sickness, proclaim, 'I am well.' In bondage, shout, 'I am free.'

I am your strength and your Provider. I am your Healer and Redeemer. I am your Deliverer.

Sorrow endured for a night, but now joy comes. The night is ending. The sun is rising. The season is changing. Wipe your tears, my child. Look. The time for rejoicing is here. From the depths of your being, sing.

Listen. Can you hear the birds? Look. Have you seen the flowers bloom? Breathe in, my beloved. My breath is in you. Sing, my loved one. My song is in you. Let courage rise. My boldness beats in your chest. Speak, child. My words are on your lips. Stretch out your hand. As I have healed you, heal. As I have delivered you, deliver. As I have provided for you, provide.

Go in my power and with my authority. Add flavour to your world. Shine my light in the dark. Show the way to the narrow path. The path that leads to life. My Spirit is in you.

Go. I am with you.

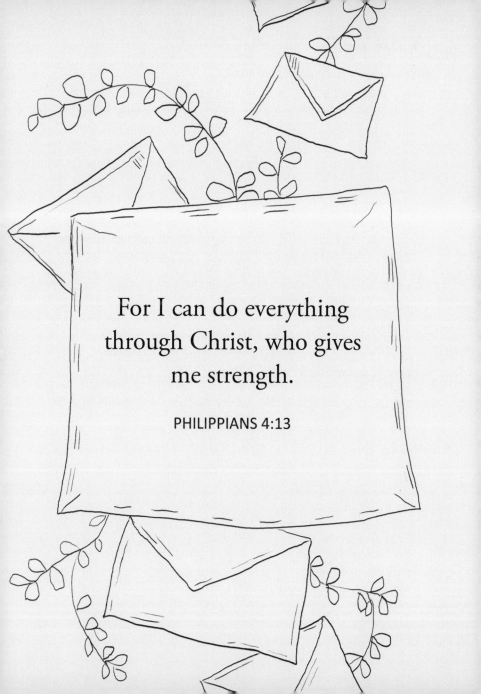

For I can do everything through Christ, who gives me strength.

PHILIPPIANS 4:13

Ask God

Where do I need courage and boldness?

Prayer

Help me lift my voice and sing to you today.

My Thoughts

A Final Note

You make my heart sing. You are my delight and I love you. My beloved, I treasure you. In you I have found favour. My righteousness is upon you. My steady arm upholds you. Highly favoured, my greatest joy. Steadfastness is your renown. Faithfulness flows from deep within.

You speak my words. You take delight in following in my footsteps and my heart rejoices. Songs flow from my lips at the thought of you. Child of faith. Firmly founded on truth. Beautiful to me. You have built your life on me and you will not be moved. My praise is on you.

Beautiful are your feet as you carry my word. Sweet are your lips as you speak my truths. Precious are your ways to me. When I look for you, I find you delighting in me. I sing over you with songs of love.

See, my people suffer for lack of knowledge. They perish in their ignorance. They seek but cannot find. They hunger but remain empty. They thirst but remain parched. They fill their belly but remain unfulfilled. Show them the way to life. Speak of me. Sing of me. Journey on, child.

I love you. I am with you. Always.

God.

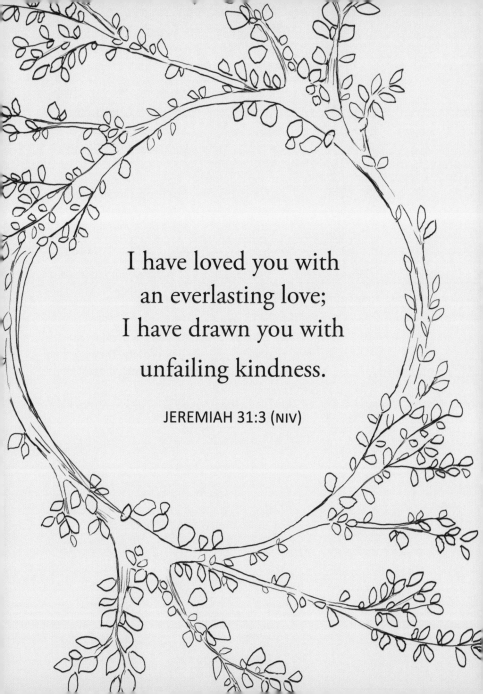

I have loved you with
an everlasting love;
I have drawn you with
unfailing kindness.

JEREMIAH 31:3 (NIV)

My Letter to God

God's Letter to Me

_____

_____

_____

_____

_____

_____

_____

_____

_____

_____

_____

_____

_____

A few people who have taught me how to be still and hear God speak

My parents, Pat and Lindsay O'Reilly, modelled quiet time with the Lord. Dad and Mom would wake up early and read the Bible, write down what they felt God was saying through his word and then pray, first on their own and then together. Thank you, Dad and Mom, for showing me how to seek God first in all things.

Pastor Ed Roebert (1939–1997) was Senior Pastor of the Hatfield Christian Church in Pretoria, South Africa. His Bible teaching on the Holy Spirit and hearing God's voice was transformative. I'm so grateful for the influence of this mighty man of God during a key time in my young Christian life.

My youth leader, Charlaine Dicks, prayed with me to receive the baptism of the Holy Spirit. It was a day that changed my relationship with God forever. In that moment, I realized that I could commune with my Maker through Jesus Christ.

About the author

Ruth O'Reilly-Smith is an experienced broadcaster and currently hosts a radio show with United Christian Broadcasters. The Bible has been key to Ruth's growth as a follower of Jesus and she is passionate about communicating God's heart through his word.

Ruth can be contacted via her website: www.ruthoreillysmith.com

Authentic

We trust you enjoyed reading this book
from Authentic. If you want to be
informed of any new titles from this author
and other releases you can sign up to the
Authentic newsletter by scanning below:

Online:
authenticmedia.co.uk

Follow us: